natural
christmas

natural christmas

TOM PRITCHARD AND
BILLY JARECKI

PHOTOGRAPHS BY TOM PRITCHARD
AND JODY RHONE

CLARKSON POTTER/ PUBLISHERS
NEW YORK

ALSO BY TOM PRITCHARD AND BILLY JARECKI

Mädderlake's Trade Secrets

Flowers Rediscovered

publisher. Published by Clarkson Potter/Publishers, 201 East 50th Street,

New York, New York 10022. Member of the Crown Publishing Group. Random

House, Inc. New York, Toronto, London, Sydney, Auckland. http://www.randomhouse.com/

CLARKSON N. POTTER, POTTER, and colophon are trademarks of Clarkson N. Potter, Inc.

Printed in China. Design by Donna Agajanian. Library of Congress Cataloging-in-Publication Data is

available upon request

ISBN 0-517-70132-4

10 9 8 7 6 5 4 3 2 1

FIRST EDITION

WE WOULD LIKE TO THANK the following for their help in making this book:

SOURCES: Brookville Nurseries, Brookville, New York; Meadowbrook Farms, Willow Grove, Pennsylvania; Bridges Nursery, Greenwich, Connecticut; Sprainbrook Nursery, Ardsley, New York; Nabel's Nursery, White Plains, New York; Holland Acres, Paramus, New Jersey; Moody Hill Tree Farms; *our flower suppliers:* Fischer & Page, Caribbean Cuts, and Dutch Flower Line.

ADDITIONAL LOCATIONS: our upstairs neighbor, Davis Given; my parents, Mr. and Mrs. J. F. Pritchard; our clients Evelyn and Leonard Lauder; our partner in the Moulin d'Olque, Joe Hardy.

For the two Christmas placemats that grace page 56, my nephew, David Tremaine.

To Mace and Minor for holding still for the best picture in the book, page 10.

To Jeffrey Gratton for the dazzling lights on page 62.

To our team at Clarkson Potter, especially our amazing designer and art director, Donna Agajanian and Jane Treuhaft; and the wonderful people who work so hard to get our books out there: Jill Cohen, Robin Strashun, Phyllis Fleiss, Joan DeMayo, Amy Boorstein, and Joan Denman. Thanks, too, to Lauren Shakely for her continuing belief in what Mädderlake has to say.

To Lew Grimes, our inventive agent.

Special thanks to Jody Rhone for his immeasurable help and gorgeous pictures; and to our close friend and special editor, Roy Finamore (assisted by Lenny Allen), for helping us make another great book.

acknowledgments

contents

IT'S NO SECRET that Christmas has become a frenzied, commercial affair, and while we, too, long for more restful times, it's the unnaturalness of it all that really bothers us. For the better part of a month, most of us shop and prepare for the big event, navigating our way through an all-too-familiar landscape of bizarrely blinking trees, plastic wreaths and garlands, and shocking displays of foil-covered poinsettia plants that look fake even if they're not. It's a season to be endured as much as enjoyed: unconvincing Santas rattle bells in our ears, malls echo with relentless holiday music, merchandise is shamelessly flogged at passersby, and while the occasional store window still charms, or a simple outdoor display causes us to pause and reflect, Christmas is often a visual jumble of artificial excess. Even the real stuff appears unnatural: precision-shaped trees that all look alike, flat balsam wreaths covered with fake holly and plastic bows, birch painted bright white (doesn't nature make them white enough?), and all manner of materials sprayed gaudy silver and gold and glued into unnatural concoctions. That's too bad, because this may be the time when we all need a little real nature the most. And while those Christmases of long ago—when trees were cut on a jaunt through the woods, and wreaths and garlands were made from greens and berries gathered along the way—may seem far, far away, a natural Christmas is still within reach, no matter where you live, if only you know what to look for and where to look.

OPPOSITE: *It's a season of anticipation for everyone—Mace and Minor anxiously await their chance to join in the fun.* ABOVE: *Old ornaments add sparkle and a sense of tradition that new ones rarely do.*

prologue

*While we rarely champion excess
for its own sake, sometimes a
lavish touch works, like
cutting amaryllis and massing them
on a candlelit mantel* (ABOVE),
*or hanging a tree with a
thousand sparkling lights* (OPPOSITE).

While Mädderlake has produced its share of extravagances over the years, we concluded long ago that the simplest, most natural settings are invariably the most appealing. In the pages that follow, Billy and I share the secrets we have discovered for creating a natural-looking Christmas at home. We began our journey far away in the wilderness refuge we discovered a few years ago in the mountains of southwestern France. With no boxes of decorations in the attic, no electricity for twinkling lights, no sidewalk lots lined with trees and wreaths, we were totally on our own. Much like that long-ago Christmas, we relied on our natural surroundings to surrender the materials to make our house festive.

Closer to home, we look back at some of the Christmases we spent in an old farmhouse nestled on the banks of a lazy river in the foothills of the Catskill Mountains. For us, this was Christmas at its easiest, with scores of local resources—roadside farmstands, mom-and-pop nurseries, colorful country markets—to sift through for the right greenery to compose a natural-looking setting. Here we share some of the techniques we learned for combining familiar materials in unusual ways.

In the final chapter, we set forth some thoughts about preparing for Christmas when you can't escape the city. This is where we decided that if you can't fight 'em, join 'em —just do it on your own terms. Never enamored of the ubiquitous poinsettia, for instance, we discovered that when plucked from the stiff and stodgy plant itself, individual flowers have an elegant bearing and can be used singly or in combination in mixed arrangements. New ways for using the materials at hand are but one way of navigating the city's surfeit of choices.

Just as the old-fashioned Christmas preparations were begun months ahead of time, we offer suggestions on how to prepare in advance so that the task does not become a last-minute struggle. There are lists of decorations and accessories to look for throughout the year, hints on planning a month in advance to find that perfect tree, where to look for a full selection of inspiring greenery and berries, and, finally, during those last frantic days, advice on collecting those plants and flowers that will add the crowning touches to your Christmas decorations.

Threaded throughout are the simple ideas that govern the settings we create. Among them are

the importance of controlling light to create a festive mood; tips on choosing tree decorations and holiday accessories; new ways to use familiar candles; and alternative sources for Christmas flowers.

Our single best counsel: keep it simple. Don't burden yourself by trying to do too much. Christmas is a season to be savored, celebrated, and shared, a time to welcome family and friends into the once-familiar surroundings you've made special for the holidays. The pages that follow show you how wonderfully easy it is to do.

GETTING READY...

what to look for
and where to look

**Flea markets, yard sales,
and antiques stores:**
old ornaments;
tree lights; tree stands;
figurative Christmas
candles (Santas, snowmen,
etc.); strings of lights;
offbeat candleholders;
antique Christmas cards and
postcards; great boxes;
old photo albums;
wrapping materials such
as ribbons, cards, tags, cord,
and twine; vases, pots,
and boxes for Christmas
plants and flowers.
**Fabric and
trimmings stores:**
wrapping materials
such as unusual ribbons,
tassels, braids, cords.
**Gift shops
and candle shops:**
fragrance-free
candles, natural piñon
and juniper incense.
**Stationery and
paper shops:**
wrapping paper,
ribbons, rubber stamps,
sturdy boxes.

Think of Christmas as a yearlong adventure and squirrel away treasures to make the holiday chores easier to handle and more fun to do. Throughout the warmer months—when you're out and about anyway—stop at yard sales, drop into antiques stores, or wander through weekend flea markets searching for ornaments, tree trimmings, wrapping materials, and accessories such as pots, vases, and candleholders.

Part of the fun of flea marketing is trying to imagine what all of that seemingly useless stuff might be good for. For years, no matter where we've looked, we've been puzzled by a lack of interesting old candleholders, so we've started creating our own. Sifting through tables of old iron tools, wooden gears, Victorian tree stands, and any other paraphernalia that might support a candle, we've come up with countless possibilities. Lots of other oddities are useful too: old photo albums and postcards can yield surprising card and tag material; bows for wreaths or packages can be found by combing through baskets of old fabric and ribbons; inexpensive boxes of all sorts—such as hatboxes, cigar boxes, wooden crates, and old grain measures—make wrapping easier, more inventive, and much more fun when the day finally comes. Remember, too, that shopping in the off season is almost always more economical than waiting until the last minute.

While many old ornaments have become pricey, bargains still abound. Sure, a handful of dealers specialize in expensive Christmas antiques, but most can't be bothered and are willing to sell off unexplored bags and boxes for a few dollars.

all through the year

Beauty, of course, is in the eye of the beholder, and each of us will have our own special radar for choosing one ornament and passing another by. Fundamental to our choices is a sense of time gone by—the suggestion of a past history as evidenced by the wear of an ornament's surface, the translucency of its finish, or the shadings of color produced by years of exposure to light and dark. Remarkable shapes, such as exotic geometric figures, fruit, pinecones, and cherubs, as well as hand-painted designs and subtle surface decorations all catch our eye.

LEFT: *Take time to sift carefully through the stacks of ornament boxes; there are almost always treasures tucked in among the more ordinary balls.*
CLOCKWISE FROM TOP: *Look for ornaments with intriguing shapes, interesting surface paints, great colors, or beautifully crazed or crackled finishes. Old figurative light bulbs are beautiful objects, but they may not work. Since there's rarely a way to test them, don't count on a glow. Examine cords, plugs, and connections carefully before buying. When they do work, old lights give off a soft, remarkable light.*

RIGHT: *An early set of tiny drummer boys fashioned out of resin and painted by hand.*
FAR RIGHT: *A half-size Santa rests on a pint-size chair.*
BELOW: *Cast-iron stocking hangers solve the age-old problem of hanging the stockings. Pretty good reproductions are available.*

offbeat ornaments

Remarkable

figured ornaments like the steely blue mushrooms (left center), the angelic little girl's face (right center), or the complicated geometric ornament (right center) make extraordinary silhouettes when suspended from a branch on the tree. Offbeat colors and interesting surface decorations are two other qualities to look for. All manner of painted surfaces abound in the ornament kingdom, but only a few— like the red and silver "beach ball" (right top)—are beautiful enough to own and cherish. While most ornaments reflect light from their shiny surfaces, balls with a worn finish or peeling paint (left bottom) have the remarkable ability to capture light and glow.

SAN : A CLAUS BRAND
TRADE MARK
Reg.
FOURTH
STAN
.S.
BA
PE
CO
RANBERRIES
NEW ENGLAND CRANBERRY SA S CO. FOR THE
ERICAN CRANBERRY EXCHANG
RK

PAT. OFF.

ARD

REL

EAT M

CHRISTMAS SNOW

Ornaments and Christmas candles make perfect little gifts to give in the weeks leading up to the big day. Instead of a bottle of wine or a bouquet of flowers, take a beautifully wrapped ornament to those seasonal get-togethers with family and friends. Keep a stash of old boxes, great little crates, and tins handy—you can pick them up for a song. Then tuck a carefully chosen ornament or candle into tissue, shredded paper, or excelsior, add a pretty ribbon, and you've got a surprising but perfectly appropriate holiday gift.

perfect little gifts

clever candleholders

Quirky candleholders add a surprising touch to candles at any time of the year. For years, we marveled at the beauty and ingenuity of old Christmas tree stands but rejected them as woefully inadequate to ever hold a tree properly. Then one day, Billy noticed that the tree trunk holes were just about the same size as the pillar candles we sold in the store, and ever since, tree stands have been our favorite Christmas candleholder.

RIGHT AND BELOW:
*Candles provide
just the right
amount of
illumination for
nooks and crannies
throughout the
house, lending an
air of richness,
sparkle, and
mystery to their
surroundings.*
FAR RIGHT: *A
treasured old Rhine
wine glass, its
stem broken, finds
new life as a
perfect holder for
a votive candle.*

remarkable candles

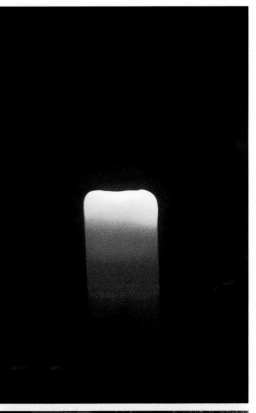

While remarkable candles add a lot more to a setting than mere light, cheap candles do little more than illuminate. Whether you're setting a holiday table, or decorating the living room or den, perfect light is one of the key ingredients to a ravishing Christmas setting. Four attributes to look for in a candle are: *glow* (right top)— great pillars reflect the glow throughout the length of the candle; *shape* (right bottom)—old Christmas candles are perfect for tiny settings; *fragrance*— real beeswax candles (left bottom) naturally smell of honey (avoid artificial fragrances); and *burn*—all of these candles burn beautifully, some transforming themselves into molten sculptures.

OVERLEAF: *Mass candles together for extraordinary effect. Use a piece of glass or mirror to protect furniture surfaces, or place candles on a platter or large, flat tray.*

christmas in the...

ICE-COATED TREES, sparkling like so many faraway diamonds in the late-afternoon sun, were all that remained of the fierce storm that had nearly sabotaged our first arrival at the *Moulin D'olque*, our new country home in France. But by day's light, the valley had returned to normal, melting the snows that had obscured our first view of the house. And then,

as we stood in the sunshine and gazed up at the glistening wonderland high overhead, it all seemed the perfect setting to preside over our first Christmas in the wilds.

This old shepherd's retreat, nestled under a precipitous line of lichen-crusted stone cliffs, was actually a compound of buildings: a house, a forge, two barns, a ruin, and a bridge, all scattered along the banks of a crystal-clear stream filled with tumbling falls and deep, cold pools. Remote might be an understatement—we had no electricity, no phone, no neighbor anywhere in view. And no traditions to draw upon for Christmas—just the most savage, splendid natural setting we'd ever encountered. So that is where we began.

With so much to do to make the house livable, we kept our decorations basic. Wreaths made of foraged material found in the nearby woods and along the steep driveway brightened

Though snowfall is a rarity for our part of France, an eerie ice storm the day before Christmas made a crystal wonderland of the trees and cliffs high above the house.

WILDS

doors and walls, while a dashing little tree harvested along the banks of the stream in back of the house added a welcome pick-me-up to the little living room. With no attic to raid, we decorated simply with clipped-on candles we'd found in a local flea market and brightly colored fruit, and thus began special new traditions of our own.

Farther afield, in the market town of the region, we came upon crowds of locals selling flowers and greens from cobbled-together tables and the trunks of their cars. Best among them were great clumps of plump, heavily berried mistletoe—not the shriveled-up little packages we often get at home—gathered by villagers from the craggy chestnut trees that border country roads, and a local holiday tradition brand new to us: clouds of bright yellow mimosa flowers, dispensed in massive bundles as fast as they could be wrapped and paid for—destined, it seems, to bring cheer and promise to local homes as the eve of the New Year drew nigh.

In the market town of Béziers, once-a-year flower vendors line the tree-shaded town square selling yellow mimosa by the armload. Scattered between the yellow piles, makeshift tables are piled high with fat, juicy clumps of locally gathered mistletoe.

These four wreaths were made from materials gathered within view
of the house: heavily berried ruscus (**ABOVE LEFT**), a native shrub that grows under the nearby
forest cover; wild rose hips (**ABOVE RIGHT**), gathered along the edges of our
precipitous driveway (center); evergreen ivy loaded with berries (**BELOW RIGHT**), harvested from
the north wall of the house; and a mixture of ivy and spruce tips (**BELOW LEFT**),
recycled from the discarded lowest branches of the Christmas tree.

gathering materials

Wildflower cutting tips: always cut from abundance, leaving sparsely growing flowers alone. Cut branches, leaves, and flowers but never remove actual plants from their native setting. Cut carefully so as not to disfigure a plant's shape, taking from all sides, not just the front. Never cut from parks, parkways, or other protected areas. Ask permission from owners before taking anything from private property.

LEFT: *A wreath made of late-blooming heathers sits amid materials gathered for the four wreaths, on page 32.* **BELOW**: *Wild blackberries—a thorny nuisance in spring and summer— yield sumptuous early fall fruit for pies and cobblers, as well as bright, colorful branches for Christmas decorations.*

Our tree had about as much personality as a tree can have. It was loose and shapely—maybe scrawny's a better description—but perfectly built to hold the old-fashioned clip-on candleholders we'd found in a local flea market. Open branching was a must to keep the candle flames away from neighboring limbs. We discovered it growing on a steep, grassy hillside halfway up the valley in back of the house, and though it looked a little stodgy where it grew, inside it was lean and beautiful. With no attic to rummage through for trimmings or decorations, we simply loaded the tree with candles, then added brightly colored clementines hung between the candles with waxed butcher's string to lend a jaunty semblance of decoration.

a tree with personality

RIGHT: *The remnants of our first Christmas celebration: though the fireplace was not yet built, portable gas heaters and an armada of candles kept the room warm and cheery.*
OPPOSITE TOP: *Fat pillar candles brought from New York illuminate a native oak wreath made earlier in the fall.*
OPPOSITE BOTTOM: *Votive candles tucked into a turn-of-the-century model train station glow on the sideboard much the way the real house does in our deep, dark valley.*

CANDLEPOWER

Located far from the electric lines that illuminate nearby hamlets and villages, we soon discovered the benefits of having to break the night's darkness with more primitive sources of light. Firelight—whether from candles, lanterns, or a glowing hearth—dances and flickers, casting shadows on the wall, reflecting in windows and on shiny surfaces, adding a cozy, old-fashioned feeling to a room or setting. But you don't have to live in the wilderness to achieve the same effect. Just turn off all the lights and let a lot of well-placed candles do the rest—you'll soon see how little it takes to totally transform a setting: scatter handfuls of votives along windowsills; use the tallest tapers you can find to dominate a table setting; place candles so that smaller ones will illuminate the outside of others.

GETTING READY...

what to look for and where to look

Nature (varies greatly by region):
wild smilax, rose hips, winterberry, hollies, laurel, snowberry, bayberry, a wealth of interesting greens.

Tree farms:
scour your area for cut-your-own-trees.

Flower shops:
in addition to the typical offerings like white pine, princess pine, English holly, heather, and balsam, most shops have access to a variety of berries and greenery such as incense cedar, rose hips, seeded eucalyptus, snowberry, pepperberry, berried juniper, pittosporum, winterberry, American holly, juniper, and noble fir branches. Ask early what can be specially ordered in your area.

Farmers' markets:
inquire about who will be bringing in natural (unsheared) trees, as well as any other special seasonal materials, such as snowberry or winterberry.

Nurseries and garden centers (varies greatly):
trees—both cut and balled-in-burlap—and a range of greenery for wreaths, garlands, and flower arrangements.

Plan ahead. Most seasonal decorating materials are pretty long-lasting, so an early start will ensure that most of the groundwork gets done before the holidays are in full swing and you're too frazzled to care. Commercial Christmas greens—those bundles of skimpy white pine roping, rows and rows of coddled trees, and especially the boxes of dreary wreaths pinned with fake holly, plastic berries, and shiny acetate bows—are, to be charitable, undistinguished, so bypass the most obvious or convenient greenery outlets in search of a more interesting and varied selection of raw materials. Remember that no matter how deft you may be at assembling them, your decorations will only be as good or as interesting as the materials that go into them.

From the absurd to the sublime, flower shops and nurseries vary wildly in their Christmas offerings, so shop around while you've got the time. Soon after Thanksgiving, we start to make the rounds of nurseries, greenhouses, garden centers, and farmers' markets to find out who will have the most interesting selections. Our best nurseries harvest a variety of unusual greens—golden cedar, Canadian hemlock with tiny pinecones, or heavily berried juniper—from their fields, grounds, and nursery stock, as well as fashion wreaths and roping from the full gamut of their yard offerings: powder-blue spruce, pyracantha, laurel, mahonia, leucothoe (fetterbush), and pachysandra.

By mid-December, we've garnered a remarkable variety of colorful greens, flowers, and berried branches, and also have a good idea where we'll be able to find a truly perfect forest tree when we're ready for it.

a month before

natural wreaths

Natural wreaths are remarkably easy to construct. Begin by creating a simple base using flexible branches such as willow, redtwig dogwood (red osier), birch, or grapevine. Using fresh branches (older ones become stiff and brittle), fashion one branch into a circle the approximate diameter of the wreath you want to create and weave the branch around itself until secure (far left). Repeat this three or four times until you have a solid frame that holds its shape and has plenty of small spaces to tuck greenery into. Cut snippets of berried branches and greens and clean the bottom inch or two for easy insertion into the wreath (bottom left). Add greens first (center top), then accents like berried juniper tips or sprigs of winterberry. For security, attach florist's wire to the wreath base and wrap the wire around the greens as you add them (center bottom). Keep rotating the wreath, adding materials to make the wreath plump and full. Insert materials in all directions (including pointing straight out and facing toward the back) to avoid a flat, pinwheel effect. Leave edges ragged for a more casual look; trim for a more formal appearance.

LEFT: *A base of wild smilax vines filled with juniper tips.*
ABOVE: *Add a great bow for a perfect finish.*

CLOCKWISE FROM UPPER LEFT:

Clusters of irregularly spaced pink and green pepperberries; a lavish quantity of dark burgundy heather tucked in all directions to make a plump, round wreath; cedar and hemlock loaded with tiny pinecones; and tea-tree branches, sparsely combined for a loose and airy look. All are built on natural twig bases.

surprising materials

CLOCKWISE FROM UPPER LEFT:
Built on a soild grapevine base, a sumptuous wreath of heavily seeded eucalyptus branches; straight out of the woods, leaves long gone, wild smilax vine loaded with shiny black berries is wound around itself until firm and full; a base of smilax garnished with snowberries; a densely layered wreath of American holly; bright red pepperberries and ivy leaves.

CLOCKWISE FROM UPPER LEFT: *Golden cedar branches; a loose juniper base with skimmia flowers and eucalyptus pods; a garland and wreath of green spruce and pinecones; pincushion protea from South Africa with waxflower from Israel; a clipped juniper base with snowberry tips; a directional version of incense cedar; mixed heathers and pepperberries; detail of flat cedar sprigs tucked into a base of redtwig dogwood; snowberry and smilax wreath in progress.*

a wreath for every door

Nothing brings a wreath down faster than a cheap-looking bow. Forget ordinary acetates and cheap flocked velvets and keep an eye out for really remarkable ribbons. Search through the Christmas shops of garden centers and seasonal stores—there's usually a handful of good choices among the more commercial ones—or check local trimmings stores, looking carefully for ribbon remnants that might be tucked away in boxes or unopened drawers. You only need a yard or so for a bow, and small remnants are often not worth displaying. So ask.

A REAL FOREST TREE

Just as a long-stemmed florist's rose says little of the garden, so, too, a cookie-cutter tree tells no tales of the woods and wilds. A Christmas tree *should* look a little scruffy and imperfect, as if it was found deep in a forest, not tidy and overly groomed. We like an irregular tree that's branched loosely enough to show a little of the trunk, with plenty of spaces between the branches begging to be laden with lights and ornaments. Think of this: most decorations hang, and therefore need ample space in which to do it. Thick, full trees force all of the decorations onto the tips of the branches and yield no spaces in which to tuck the twinkling lights and shiny balls that add depth and mystery, making a natural tree magical looking.

OPPOSITE: *Look for a shapely tree with a view of the trunk and plenty of space between branches for hanging ornaments and dangling lights.*

In many parts of the country, cut-your-own tree farms offer the best, if not the only, chance of finding a real forest tree. Bundling everyone up against the chill wind and tramping through the snow in search of that perfectly shaped tree affords an adventure friends and family can share together. It's a great opportunity to spend some time getting reacquainted with the woods and wilds, and a time to see if democracy really works, as one opinion after another is weighed in the search for consensus. Best of all, harvesting a tree and hauling it home adds a memorable new story to the unfolding tales of the Christmas season.

Ninety percent of all Christmas trees are meticulously groomed through a practice called shearing. Commercial tree farmers lop off the tip ends of their evergreens, much the way hedges are manicured, to create "perfectly shaped" trees. Shearing also produces thicker foliage and more uniform branch spacing, closing up the natural interior spaces of each tree—witness the dense, fat Scotch pines and Douglas firs that eventually dominate the tree lots. According to industry statistics, this practice has pretty much been consumer driven—answering a need for uniformity and perfection, perhaps, or maybe the silly idea that perfectly groomed trees are perceived to have cost more and therefore have more "value." While commercially farmed trees all look the same, natural trees—those you might have come across in the woods somewhere—are individual in appearance, each a reflection of the particular spot in which it grew.

ABOVE: *Without the charm of a naturally shaped tree, this selection is at least sparsely branched enough to hold decorations adequately.* ABOVE RIGHT: *Like flowers, trees need water to keep their needles refreshed. Re-saw the trunk within an hour or two of securing in the tree holder. Keep the reservoir filled.* RIGHT: *A close-up of a sheared spruce dramatizes the damage. Tip ends are broken and scarred; interior space is closed up.*

Buying a commercial tree

If you're lucky, you'll find a section of unsheared balsams—probably the cheapest trees on the lot— with natural, irregularly spaced branches and lichen-covered trunks. The rest will probably be sheared. Avoid trees with upturned-branches, such as Scotch pines and white spruces— they're hard to decorate— and look for trees with branches that extend out or hang down, such as noble fir, or green and blue spruces. Pass the thickest trees by and look for trees with a little more interior space. Don't be obsessed with perfection. Remember, a one-sided tree will fit better up against a wall or in a corner.

ABOVE: *Unsheared trees provide ample spaces to tuck ornaments.* **RIGHT**: *A fabulous spruce with a double top has an extraordinary ragged shape and soft, pendant branches. See a photograph of this tree decorated on page 86.*

Don't toss your tree away after the holidays; instead, return it to nature. Many communities—usually through the city parks department—set up recycling centers to shred de-tinseled trees into mulch and compost. Participants in the program are encouraged to take mulch home for use in their gardens. In cities without this service, contact your local department of sanitation for tree pickup schedules.

OPPOSITE: *Cut (with permission) from an abandoned landscape nursery, this remarkable Siberian spruce sports wild, rangy limbs with ample room for lights and decorations. A photograph of this tree decorated is on page 85.* **RIGHT:** *Trees litter the streets of New York City after New Year's Day awaiting a special garbage detail for removal.*

recycling trees

christmas in the...

SNOW DEVOURED the countryside that Christmas, a huge, soft, wet snow that swallowed up yard and drive and created a masterpiece of the towering spruce we'd wired to the edge of the picket fence. Our beautiful stone house was a storybook setting, and creating Christmas, reenacting familiar traditions and inventing new ones, was always an easygoing adventure shared with family and friends. We had learned long ago that coming to the country meant leaving the city and its excesses behind. Shopping at the roadside farmstands, nurseries, and old-time markets is part of the flavor of rural life. Exploring these places for the natural ingredients we favored for wreaths and garlands, or searching for that perfect woodsy tree that would cozy into a corner of the living room, was no exception.

Whereas Christmas in the wilds can be a struggle, and Christmas in the city may offer a surfeit of choices that needs to be carefully culled through, the rural countryside is probably the perfect venue for creating an old-fashioned Chrsitmas. Gardens, adjacent woods, and fields are filled with berried branches—wild roses laden with burgundy rose hips, jet-black berry clumps hanging from smilax vines, or powder-blue clusters of bayberries; farmstands and nurseries

abound with locally gathered holly branches, boxes of offbeat wreath-making materials, and shapely trees; and greenhouses are filled with an array of brightly colored plants to buy and cut from.

A cut tree was tied to the fence and hung with outdoor lights. A soft, wet snow transformed the yard and gardens into a perfect Christmas setting.

COUNTRY

Heather—one of the few flowers that can hold its own out of water—is a perfect material for wreaths and garlands. Depending on the season, heathers vary from cream and white through a full range of pale to dark reds and purples. Look for fresh, firm flower clusters that don't shed when you shake them. Many heather varieties will retain their color even as they dry.

OPPOSITE: Working clockwise around a wire wreath form, enough heather was attached to completely cover the form; into this base, additional heather was wedged in various directions to make the wreath plump and full. **THIS PAGE:** *Garnishing the mantel couldn't have been easier. Bereft of their leaves—used to make the garland—the leftover pittosporum branches were spaced along the back of the mantel to serve as holders for the remaining heather. An eclectic collection of candles and old cloth figurines—Tiny Tim, Scrooge, and some inebriated carolers among them—were tucked in wherever they looked good.*

We're always on the lookout for new materials that add an interesting twist to traditional decorations. While foraging in the cooler of a local florist one Christmas, we spied a bucket filled with tall branches of waxy-leafed pittosporum, a landscape plant used in the warmer parts of the country and a staple of florists everywhere. Once the branches were cut up into 10-inch lengths, Billy began wiring one to another, securing each stem to the next with a roll of green florist's wire. Start with a sturdy piece, then lay in the second, about halfway along the length of the first. Fasten well, then wind the wire around both stems and lay in a third, continually wrapping the wire around the stems to bind them together into a continuous rope. The leaves of each new piece will hide the wire. Using a continuous wire, keeping the spacing relatively short, and always binding well will ensure a strong, solid garland. Then, look for new places to add a festive holiday touch. A couple of bright bows help this leftover piece of garland (opposite) dress up a corner of the dining room.

garlands

CUTTING FROM PLANTS

Life in the country has many charms, but an abundant selection of interesting fresh flowers isn't one of them. Over the years, we've learned to make the rounds of greenhouses and flower shops in search of seasonal plants from which to cut. Cyclamen, Rieger begonias, calamondin oranges, Jerusalem cherry, jasmine, and azaleas—all fairly common in most parts of the country—readily lend their foliage and flowers to festive table arrangements. Some flowers—cyclamen, for example—look dramatically fresh and different when free of their usual bed of greens. Others—such as Rieger begonias and azaleas—can be cut up or cut from. Combined with other flowers, or simply rearranged, they become a fresh flower tour de force.

OPPOSITE TOP:
*Freed from their pots
and tucked into
a pair of champagne
flutes, cyclamen
flowers take on
a whole new
character.* **OPPOSITE
BOTTOM:** *A mix
of red begonias
makes a simple but
festive table
arrangement.* **LEFT:**
*Rieger begonias,
cyclamen, and
branches of red
kalanchoe combine
to make an elegant,
natural centerpiece.*
ABOVE: *A miniature
pineapple harvested
from a nursery
plant rests rakishly
in an American
pottery vase.*

MIXING OLD AND NEW
Few things invoke such a flood of memories as trimming the country tree. Out of sight and mute for most of the year, decorations and ornaments freed from their attic prison and considered for the new tree instantly conjure up scenes and stories from Christmases past. While many people strive to create "theme trees," collecting only angels, or all gold objects, or blending the ornaments perfectly with the surrounding decor, we prefer a totally eclectic mix. Our collection includes homemade painted dough ornaments made twenty years ago with friends, some remarkable antiques found over the years, recycled cards and tags from presents past, and a handful of amusing dollhouse props—a frying pan, a croquet set, tennis rackets, a shiny silver radiator—recently discovered at a craft and hobby store. Newly acquired treasures or even silly little objects found during the course of the year help keep the Christmas story growing, ensuring that each new tree will feel warm and personal, the best you've ever had.

OPPOSITE: Figurative candles are among the best flea-market finds. **ABOVE:** *A complicated mix of decorations makes a tree fun to explore.* **BELOW:** *An old-fashioned tree is laden with ornaments and alive with lights.* **LEFT:** *Dollhouse miniatures found in a national crafts chain make perfectly quirky new ornaments.*

RIGHT: *While regular strands of lights are best woven along the limbs of the tree, accent lights— such as these jewel-like lanterns—can be strung from branch to branch as a feature rather than a background.* **OPPOSITE:** *A diminutive papier-mâché Santa holds a sack full of tiny ornaments.* **ABOVE AND BELOW:** *Shiny ornaments catch and reflect light.*

dazzling lights

OPPOSITE AND ABOVE: *Torn fragments photocopied from a cherished childhood book,* Tommy in Topsyturvyland, *make a box that's worth saving forever. Shredded paper recycled from a mail-order amaryllis delivery festively protected the contents, while a bingo card "tag" found at an antiques market in France added the perfect finish.* **LEFT:** *Gorgeous bows are easy to make—just start with a great piece of ribbon.* **BELOW:** *A plastic sleeve protected this tiny plant while it was nestled in its homemade box.*

Good commercial papers are expensive, and, at least for some of us, any paper is unmanageable when it comes to enclosing gifts. I've never been able to wrap anything, so Billy came up with this foolproof technique. Start with a sturdy box—sweater and shoe boxes are perfect—and a pile of images copied or clipped from books, magazines, or old prints and photographs. Next, spray the back of each sheet with a thin coating of spray adhesive, available from art supply, craft, or stationery stores. Apply one after the other, butting or overlapping images as you see fit, carefully turning corners, wrapping the lids, and covering inside surfaces too. Add a ribbon and the deed is done.

homemade packages

GETTING READY...

Time for the real show! All the groundwork lining up the best resources finally pays off. Keep open to the possibilities as you roam around greenhouses and flower shops: anything that's growing can yield a branch or a few flowers for a centerpiece or large arrangement; anything that's snowy white or bright red can have total Christmas appeal.

We start with the best nurseries and garden centers, searching out unusual plants such as ardisia crispa (with its cluster of tree-like stems, waxy green leaves, and bright red berries), flowering jasmines, and fruited citrus plants. In addition to the miniature calamondin oranges, many greenhouses carry a winter stock of lemons, limes, oranges, and grapefruits whose heady fragrance puts artificial scents to shame.

Don't hesitate to cut from plants. These Christmas crops have been produced specifically to brighten up holiday settings. For those with space and a green thumb, think of holiday plants as an investment with a future: even those severely pruned will eventually regenerate and produce another round of cutting possibilities. Remember to pass the tight, compact plants by—there's no stem length to cut from—and choose the looser ones: the leggiest azaleas, Rieger begonias with the tallest flowers, the most fully blooming cyclamen.

As you work with flowers and foliage cut from plants, vary the balance of green to flower to suit the setting: looser, leafier arrangements are more casual looking, while tighter, more flowery mixes are much more formal. Be lavish in your choices.

the final days

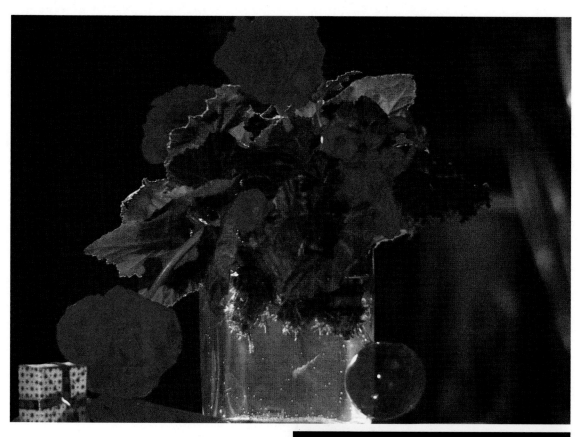

PRECEDING PAGES: *An adventurous pastiche of seasonal materials arranged in a rectangular glass vase. Cut from plants: leggy azalea branches, miniature roses, amaryllis, and a whole calamondin orange plant. Found in the flower market: forced quince branches, hybrid lilac, and jazzy red and yellow gloriosa lilies.*
ABOVE: *Its roots washed and wedged in a narrow vase, a brilliant red double begonia looks fresh and quirky.*
RIGHT: *Clusters of vallota flowers, red enough to be a perfect Christmas candidate.*

new christmas flowers

Cut from offbeat **tropical plants,**
this spirited holiday centerpiece—
a mix of Jerusalem cherry, confederate
jasmine, and mistletoe fig—was a snap to
make. Begin with a great container—
like this snow-crested McCoy planter—cut a
block of florist's foam to fit snugly,
attach it to the container with green florist's
tape, and soak thoroughly. Then
add fig branches, rotating the container and
varying the direction of each new
piece. Fill out with Jerusalem cherry and
add accents of jasmine to finish.

When the container is clear, we prefer not to use florist's foam. Form a natural flower-holder instead. First wedge a branch into the container, then run a strip of florist's tape along the rim, making a loop around the branch to fasten the branch to the edge. Repeat with a second branch placed in the opposite direction. Tuck flowers into the supporting structure, rotating the container as you work.

RIGHT: Since ingredients are sparse, leave bottom foliage on azalea cuttings to better lodge into the openings between the quince branches. **BELOW:** *Poinsettia flowers add the crowning touch.*

The poinsettia had never appealed to us until we decided to explore its potential as a cut flower resource. Lo and behold, cutting from a plant and using it in an untraditional way once again freed up a flower to become something fresh and new. Combine cut poinsettias with other flowers (opposite), use singly in small-necked vases, or mass a few together to create a special Christmas arrangement.

ABOVE: *Sear poinsettia stems in an open flame or dip in boiling water to seal the sap inside the stem and double the life of the flower.* **LEFT**: *Four flowers sit majestically in a footed vase.*

Amaryllis are dramatically shaped, easy to grow, easy to give, and blazing with a full range of vivid Christmas reds—from the perfect claret of "Mahogany" and the sizzling pink of "Bolero," to the subtly striped "Apple Blossom" and the sprightly tinged "Picotee." Although some markets are finally beginning to offer cut amaryllis, we often buy bulbs from catalogs and grow our own to ensure availability for a certain event, or to have some of the hard-to-find varieties. A recent favorite, the miniature "Scarlett Baby," is pictured here in a variety of guises.

CLOCKWISE FROM UPPER LEFT: *Variations on a theme: A full knot of flowers squeezed into an urn-shaped footed vase. Pared-down flowers and leaves casually placed in a pilsner glass. A couple of flowers tumble off the rim of a pewter sugar bowl. A highbrow silver vase dresses up the same flowers. "Red Peacock" and "Pasadena" double amaryllis await cutting.*

Anatomy of a centerpiece

Tape florist's foam into a low dish
and soak it well. Cover the foam with leaves
cut from a cyclamen, varying their
direction and allowing them to drape over the
edges. If stems are thin, poke holes in the
foam with a nail or chopstick. Add flowers cut
from a miniature rose, leaving some
foliage on each stem. Remember to rotate the
container as you work. Fill in with mandevilla
flowers and foliage, and top it off
with accents of cut cyclamen.

Rieger begonias are perfect
candidates for cutting. Useful in a variety of
settings from table centerpieces to bud vases,
these hybrid begonias offer a rich array
of colors to choose from: deep pink and peach to
pale yellow and butterscotch to brilliant
vermillion. Flowers vary too; both single and double
blossoms come in clear jewel-tone colors
or subtle, complex shadings.

CLOCKWISE FROM UPPER LEFT: *A moss-
covered pot of begonias straight from the
greenhouse. Two flower clusters amid carefully
placed leaves spell total elegance. A lavish
cluster of flowers casually nestled into a
pottery vase.*

White Christmas Resembling
piles of wet snow caught in a barberry bush,
these white azalea flowers have been
transformed by vase and setting. We cut the
longest branches from a thick, full plant,
thinned them out, then reconfigured them into a
loose, irregular shape, allowing plenty of
room to show off the remarkable container.
Azaleas are as versatile as begonias, working
equally well in table centerpieces, in mixed
arrangements, or as individual cut flowers.

PRECEDING PAGES: *Markets
everywhere are filled to overflowing with
lushly grown Christmas azaleas. Search out
interesting plants—standard or topiary
forms, for instance—then repot them in
something festive to give as gifts or brighten
a corner of the house.*

christmas in the...

FIRE IN ALL ITS GUISES—a hearth ablaze with dancing flames atop a glowing bed of embers; a yule log burning slowly through all the days of the season; an animated procession of red and green votives flickering along a mantel or illuminating a festive holiday table; an assortment of candles glowing in a darkened corner of the room—is one of the two essential ingredients that can make magic of a Christmas setting in the city. Even if you don't have a traditional hearth to gather around, turning the lights down low and letting the soft glow of flickering candlelight transform a room can evoke just as much of the warm, cozy spirit that a fireplace does.

The other essential key to a magical Christmas in the city: find and transport some pieces of the natural countryside and the wilds into strategic places in your house or apart- ment. People who live far from the shadows of narrowly spaced buildings and closely gridded streets see fields and meadows and forests every day, but the rest of us don't. Christmas is a perfect opportunity, if only for a moment or two, to redress the balance. Thus the choices of tree and greenery become heightened in the city, and demand even more care when making your selection. When choosing a tree, think big and allow the tree to dominate the room. A perfectly grand Christmas

OPPOSITE: *A few well-chosen greens and colored votives scattered along the mantel quickly transform the room into a cheery Christmas setting.*

CITY

tree, one that brings a real taste of the woods and the forest into view, is the best means any city dweller has by which to experience firsthand—to re-create, in fact—a little of that nature that is so sadly missing.

Keep the hot glue gun in a drawer, forget the heavily laden magnolia garlands sprayed gold and hung with bows and fruit, the banks of poinsettia plants, towers of sugared fruit, the tinsel-tossed tree that is far more metallic than green. Nature is the goal. If anything, the surfeit of choices a city has to offer demands an editor's eye, to pare away extraneous choices until a perfectly simple solution is at hand. Choose the most evocative greenery you can find: rugged noble fir branches; garlands of eucalyptus, juniper, and cedar; soft blue-gray sprays of spruce and coral-leaved barberry. Sift through the myriad flower choices; the seductive clivia flowers, the red nerine lilies that smell like chocolate, the subtle blossoms of witch hazel, and select only those

that totally appeal. Then use them in a simple, straightforward way to enhance the natural attributes of your setting.

The Christmas seasons we've spent in New York City, a little more elegant and polished than those in the country, with a little more razzle-dazzle perhaps, at heart have only one goal: to transform our rooms for a while, create a little magic, change the scenery to evoke as best we can the essence of the faraway countryside and memories of the distant wilds.

LEFT: *Far from the storybook versions, this city snowman reflects the quirky personalities of the Greenwich Village residents who made him.*
OPPOSITE: *Bayberry branches bought at the farmers' market and wired to our front window grill add a wintry silhouette to our view of the street.*

Trimming a tree:

The larger the tree, the more secure it will need to be. Wedge the tree into the stand and adjust the leveling screws until the tree is vertical. For added peace of mind, wire the tree to nearby moldings. Lay in the lights first, taking care to hide strands along natural branch and trunk lines. Keep interior spaces free for ornaments and trimmings. Use lights liberally inside the tree so the trunk and interior spaces are well lit and the tree glows from within. If the tree is placed in a corner or against a wall, don't neglect its back; lights placed there will help define the fullness of the tree. If you're adding ornaments, start from the top and work down. Mix ornaments of different sizes together, hanging some in clusters, scattering others individually. Hang heavy ornaments from a firm branch; attach delicate ornaments to branch tips.

RIGHT: *Trimming the tree is one of the best of Christmas experiences. Include friends and family; serve champagne, sherry, or hot cocoa and make it a party.* OPPOSITE: *The tree in our upper parlor was so naturally beautiful this year that, once we lit it, we decided not to load it down with ornaments.*

little touches

Some of the most charming Christmas flourishes
are also the tiniest. Use leftover flowers and greens and create
a few vignettes in out-of-the-way places—there's always
a place or two in the kitchen, on a bedside table, dresser, or
bathroom vanity—and spread the cheer around.

OPPOSITE: *Little cuttings from azalea plants,*
loosely tucked into colorful Victorian
pony glasses and bathed in candlelight, reflect
themselves in a small mirror ringed with
flat-needled cedar and berried juniper tips.
CLOCKWISE, THIS PAGE: *A wintry arrangement uses*
star-of-Bethlehem and a couple of spruce tips left
over from the dining room mantel. The tree's not the only
place for ornaments. Scatter some around the table,
or fill a glass bowl and brighten up a dark
corner of the room. A single sprig of jasmine happily
mingles with old Christmas candles in the cubbyholes
of a vintage secretary in the living room.

festive mantels

OPPOSITE: *An opulent array of sugared fruit nestled among white pine, Casablanca and calla lilies, French tulips, hybrid lilac, Queen Anne's lace, and euphorbia fulgens matches the grandeur of the setting.*
CLOCKWISE, THIS PAGE: *Votives displace tapers on a flea-market candelabra. As the season progresses tuck in fresh flowers to charge the setting for a special occasion. White azalea are joined by plump blue-spruce branches to liven up the dining room.* OVERLEAF: *A natural mantel is easy to create: place greens loosely—in this case cedar and hemlock branches—then fill in with beautiful fruit and candles.*

index